The Grease
Guide To Coolness

an armand eisen/thomas durwood publication

Ariel  Books

distributed by Ballantine Books

The

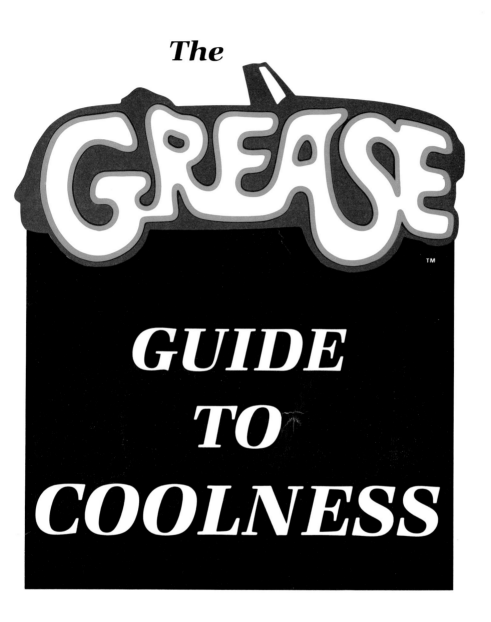

GREASE ™

GUIDE
TO
COOLNESS

**Edited by
Armand Eisen**

**Written by
Joe Kelly**

INTRODUCTION

Do You Really Want To Be Cool?

Cool is not for everyone. It can lead to academic failure, knife fights in church, maybe even prison. So beware!

Aren't You Tired Of Being A Nerd?

How does it feel to sit home alone polishing the ceiling while cool guys and gals are out dancing, rumbling, making out, dragging, and drinking, all this every night of the week, including Monday.

Is It Hard To Be Cool?

It used to be, but this book makes it easy. Danny Zuko, the coolest guy of them all, is right here telling you guys and gals how to be cool. He even answers personal letters. Danny takes you through the movie "Grease" and tells you exactly why he and his friends are so cool. For those of you who can read, we have a 1950's dictionary of **Cool** words. For those of you who can't, there is a step by step visual section showing how the average Nerd (like yourself) is transformed into a guy almost as cool as Danny. We also have a guide to dating and an advertising section full of cool products.

When Will I Be Cool?

Being cool, like anything worthwhile, takes time. We do not intend to promise anything but miracles. If, however, you are dissatisfied in any way and do not feel 100% cooler after reading this book, please return it personally before July, 1960, to the Russian Embassy in Anchorage, Alaska. They will cheerfully give you a complete refund — no questions asked!

The Grease Guide to Coolness

No part of this book may be reproduced by any means without prior written consent from the publisher: Ariel Books, Suite 2406 Power & Light Bldg., Kansas City, Mo. 64105. This edition is distributed in the United States by Ballantine Books, a division of Random House, Inc., New York, and simultaneously in Canada by Ballantine Books of Canada, Ltd., Toronto, Canada.

ISBN 0-345-27888-7
Library of Congress #78-65035
Manufactured in the U.S.A.
First Edition — October, 1978

Acknowledgements

Design Consultant Gary Britt.

Special thanks to Craig Kelly, Frank McMahan, Deborah Carberry, Scott Smith, Celeste Welch, Lisa Goetz, Dave McGuire, Joseph & Kathleen Kelly.

Vintage cars were provided by John Joslin, Lloyd Roland & Mark Buehlin.

Photographs pages 50–80 by Joe Kelly.

CONTENTS

In Cool We Trust

Danny Zuko's helpful hints on cool clothes, cars and dancing. If he can do it, why can't you?

Letters To Danny Zuko

Danny answers your personal letters on all aspects of coolness (for a nominal fee, of course!)

1959: Fact Or Fantasy?
A Dictionary Of The 50's

What was really happening . . . if anything . . . in 1959?

From Nerd To Greaser
In Six Easy Steps

Through a two year, nationwide search our staff has located America's biggest Nerd. Employing a simple step-by-step process, we transform our loser into a totally cool delinquent.

A Guide To Dating

A pictorial essay documenting cool and uncool dating behavior. A young couple's search for sixth base is analyzed.

Advertising

Our loyal sponsors who have made all this possible.

IN COOL WE TRUST

In which Danny Zuko gives you a guided tour of the movie **GREASE** to tell you all about . . .

Cool Clothes

Cool Hair

Cool Cars

Cool Dancing

Cool Sports

Cool Clothes

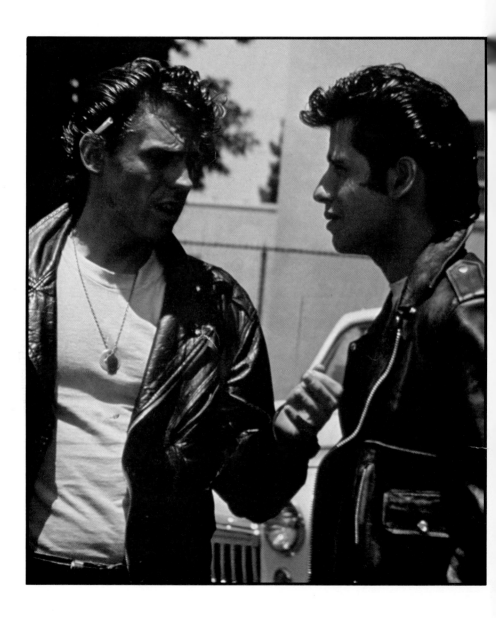

T-Shirts

It's important for girls to be feminine and lady-like. Get a look at these coordinated pink bus jackets — far out, huh — very refined. This is the way to dress for you girls who are going all the way.

You'll never be out of style in a white T-Shirt.

Bow Ties?

This guy may make straight A's in American Citizenship 101 but he'd get an F— in cool school. Like bow ties are strictly for French poodles. He'll be lucky if he lasts 20 minutes in reform school.

How about these cheerleaders? I bet they all got left with the check at the drive-in. If you dress wholesome like that, you're bound to get stood up.

Plastic Pants

Now look at my friend in black. She really knows how to dress cool. If you gals dress like that you'll have dates, parties & romance every day of the week. Guys will call you up three months in advance to go to the drive-in. Get yourself some plastic pants and you'll never be alone again. These are the pants of the future; by the 1970's everyone will be wearing them.

Cool Hair

Kiss Kirl

Perfect hair grooming does the trick here. It's the easy way to impress a gal. The Kiss Kirl is Keen, but takes years of practice with a comb to perfect. I wouldn't recommend it to a beginner. I've been practicing for five years at least.

These plastic flowers are wild. They always look fresh and only need occasional watering.

Blonde Wigs

Here's Riz wearing a blonde wig and a purple shirt. Looks like she's practicing to get Elvis' attention at next Friday's concert — she wants to get invited backstage. She'll be lucky if she's not picked up by the F.B.I. for illegally impersonating Sandra Dee!

Sandy's old hairstyle is simply dullsville!

Pink Dye

Look at the difference Sandy's new hairstyle makes. It's a cinch she'll be having more fun, her grades will go down, her parents will be up late every Friday and Saturday night worrying. She may even run away from home or get thrown in jail.

Look at Frenchy's casual and attractive pink hair style. Already she is the center of attention.

Cool Cars

Here I demonstrate proper driving position. The left hand rests loosely on the steering wheel. Eyes look down to check for squirrels blocking the road. The right hand is kept free at all times to help the passenger keep her dress on. Swept back hair adds 3 mph. to the top speed. With this look, the highway is all yours. Other drivers pull off the road to let you pass, friendly police-men wave you through speed traps. Life is easy when you're cool.

Tail Fins

Tailfins win friends and in-fluence people. I couldn't live without at least two pairs. The clear plastic hood allows constant monitoring of the oil level, drives the chicks crazy.

Here's where a convertible top helps you get out in a hurry. It's the perfect thing for a rumble.

Cool Dancing

Squids?

Here is where knowing how to dance really comes in handy. Sandy and I have got the whole crowd impressed. If we get lucky we may win two free tickets to the new 3-D movie, "Giant Killer Squids from Outer Space." Now that's far out.

Cha-Cha is really kicking up her heels here. She is doing her best to win a dream-date with King Farouk — can you blame her?

Cool Sports

Attitude

Look how impressed that coach is by my cool attitude. I've got him really snowed. He's sure to give me a varsity letter before I even try out. I many not even have to go to practice, just because I'm cool. You can do it too!

My relaxed attitude intimidates the pitcher. Home runs become as easy as stealing hubcaps.

Letters to

Danny Zuko

In which Danny personally answers your letters on all but the
most intimate topics.

Of Course You're A Nerd!

We know it, Danny knows it, Sandy knows it, even your folks know it. But **you** want to change and you do need help. **That** is what Danny is here for.

Is There Any Hope?

Of course there is hope; as long as you have sent $15 with each letter, there is plenty of hope.

What Should I Do?

Exactly what he tells you, no more, no less. Remember, he's been acting cool for years.

Dear Danny,

I've got this groovy new boyfriend. He's the manager of the chess team. My folks first met him at church last week. They were very upset to see him wearing his coonskin cap in church. They just don't understand that he has got to wear it everywhere.

You see, he is trying to break the world's record for continuous wearing of a coonskin cap. Right now the record is 8 years, 3 months, and 4 days. Billy only has 2 years, 1 month and 3 days before he has the world's record. He can't quit now – just to please my folks.

My folk's won't let him in the house with his cap on. They don't understand how important that record is to Billy. What should I do to help them understand and accept my boyfriend?

Faith from Ocean City

Dear Faith,

Have him put a live chicken on top of his hat for a week. Your folks will be so relieved when he gets rid of the chicken that they won't even notice the coonskin anymore.

Danny

Dear Danny,

Ever since my Dad bought that foreign car dealership, I've been down in Dullsville. He made me sell my far out '48 Chevy. That car had everything — three on the tree, beer barrel carb, simulated chrome steering wheel spinner and a stolen super modified Sam Eggbeater special under the hood.

Worst of all man, he makes me drive this cheap foreign job which looks like a cockroach squished by a spiked heel. Trying to make out with Sally Sue in that crate is like trying to play baseball in the closet. Even worse, it won't climb the hill up to Lover's Lane unless I get out and push.

My Dad owns Bob's Import Emporium of Fershlinger, Ohio. He will throw me out if he ever catches me driving an American car. How should I keep the car that I'm driving and still be cool?

Patriot

Dear Patriot,

Put some fins on your Cheap Foreign Car. I know a guy in Mountain View, Kansas who can do it for you cheap.

P.S. Also, try making out in the closet and playing baseball in the car.

Danny

Dear Danny,

I have a terrible problem. This horrible gang of teenage ruffians called the "Iron Poodles" is tormenting me, wherever I go. I'm president of the student council, a lead tenor for the glee club and the trainer for the chess team, yet these fellows show me absolutely no respect.

When I go home from school, this awful, horrible, wicked gang of teenage lechers, bullies and ruffians follows me home. They wait until I get in front of my girlfriend's house and then they rush out and begin beating me up all over my body and face. A week ago, they stole a sack of fish fertilizer and forced me to eat all of it before they would let me go home to Mother. Yesterday it was even worse. They made me get down on my hands and knees and pretend I was a sheep. My girlfriend saw it and is now too embarrassed to speak to me. I've got to prove to everyone that I'm a man and not a sheep. How can I get that horrible gang to stop tormenting me?

Wolf in Sheep's Clothing

Dear Wolf,

Next time they follow you, pretend you are a turkey or maybe even a chinchilla. They'll be looking so hard for the sheep, they won't even notice you. Fershlinger? Isn't that in Ohio?

Danny

Dear Danny,

The other day I found out that Leroi was messing around with my steady, Cindy. I told that jerk, "I don't want you seeing Cindy, I don't want you talking with Cindy, I don't even want you thinking about Cindy."

I don't quite know what happened, but the next day Cindy came up to me in the lunch room and said, "Frank, I don't want to see you, I don't want to talk to you, I don't even plan to think about you." Guess I did something wrong, huh?

I felt pretty bad about it until I went out and "borrowed" the school bus and parked it in her front yard. That sure showed her.

I've been going out with Ann, Leroi's old girl. The only problem is I got this tatoo on my chest and it doesn't say "I love Ann;" it says "I love Cindy." I've also got it tatooed on the soles of my feet. When Ann and I went to the beach, I was so afraid to show her my tatooes, that I kept my shirt and shoes on when we went swimming. She is beginning to think I'm weird and demands to see my chest and feet. What should I do?

Ready for Winter

Dear Ready,

Why don't you have " 's Chicken Restaurant" tatooed after "I love Cindy." Tell Ann that you worked as a human billboard last summer with your "I love Cindy's Chicken Restaurant" tatoo. Don't take off you socks, she'll never believe it if she sees your feet.

Danny

Dear Danny,

I'm a senior at a private all boys school. I'm a very fine actor; everyone says so. I always get the lead roles. My only problem is that the role I get is always the female lead. I sure don't know why. My mother thinks it's because I wear pink stretch pants to school. I personally think they look very masculine.

Whenever they see me, the football players make cruel and unusual gestures. Even this weird transfer student, who thinks he's a chinchilla, calls me, "Juliet." I've become such a laughing stock that I can't even get a date with Wendy "Watermelons" Jones anymore.

How can I get a more masculine and cool image? I want to play Romeo in the Spring play.

Romeo

Dear Juliet – I mean, Romeo,

Why don't you transfer to an all girls school? They'll let you play the male lead for sure. By the way: is that guy who thinks he's a chinchilla from Fershlinger?

Danny

The head cheerleader of Orange Grove, Alaska writes:

Danny,

Please send me some pictures of you. I just love your far-out hair and clothes!!!

Call Collect

Dear Collect,

Doesn't everyone?

Danny

A romantic junior from Mountain View, Kansas writes:

Dear Danny,

I finally got this guy I've been chasing for weeks to go steady with me. He's not even in school or anything. He works in a custom bodyshop that puts tailfins on Volkswagons. In five more years he's going to be the assistant manager.

He's really a cool guy. You should see the lizard skin upholstery in his car. He oils it every day to keep it shiny.

Things were going great until he joined this horrible gang called the "Killer Parakeets." They spend all their spare time mooning the Retired Ladies for a Decent America. It's horrible; two of the ladies have died of fright, (this week alone)! How can I get him started on a different hobby?

Worried in Mountain View

Dear Worried,

Get him interested in picking on someone his own age. I know a guy in Fershlinger who thinks he's a chinchilla. He loves to be entertained by gangs. I'll give you his address.

Danny

Dear Danny,

My girlfriend, Susie, won't hardly talk to me anymore. All she can think about is your hair. I can't believe it. She has even wall papered the interior of her parents car with pictures of you. What should I do?

Jealous in Orange Grove

Dear Jealous,

Give her my phone number.

Danny

Dear Danny,

My folks left town last week to visit my deceased Uncle Fred. They left me with their '51 Cadillac and told me to take real good care of it. I was getting sort of bored and depressed on Friday night; my girlfriend had just dumped me for a traveling leather socks salesman. I thought that since I had nothing better to do, I would just go on down to Thunder Road and watch the grudge matches. Wouldn't you know it, I met this weird kid from Fershlinger, Ohio. He was showing off his brand new Chevy. It's got everything from a steering wheel spinner to chrome tires. He started egging me on and before I knew it I had agreed to race him for the owner's papers. I gave him a pretty good race considering I forgot to release the parking brake. It was close, but I lost my folk's brand new Cadillac. I'm sure scared of telling them the bad news.

Do you think I should run away from home? I'm thinking about taking my parent's mobile home and going to Vegas to see if I can win enough to buy them a new car.

Heading for Vegas

Dear Heading,

Head back home. Bet that guy that your parent's mobile home is faster than his Chevy. And when you're driving it, remember to take the parking brake off.

Danny

Dear Danny,

I've got this really neat new boyfriend. He works as a bouncer at a senior citizens recreational center. Things were going really good until we went to the beach. When we went swimming, he wouldn't take either his shirt or his shoes off. He said it was because he was cold.

The other day I demanded to see him without his shirt or his shoes. I couldn't believe it—he had, "I love Cindy's Chicken Restaurant" tatooed on his chest. He said he worked as a human billboard last summer. I believed him, until he showed me the soles of his feet. He had the same thing tatooed there. He said a famous friend of his told him it was cool to have "I love Cindy's Chicken Restaurant" tatooed on the soles of the feet. What kind of fool would give advice like that?

Angry Edith

Dear Angry,

It sure sounds terrible, but you should count your blessings — it could be a lot worse. Just today another girl from your home town wrote in to tell me that someone had advised her boyfriend to pretend he was a chinchilla.

Danny

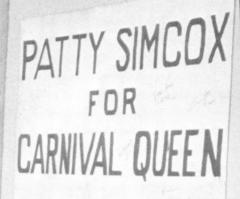

1959: FACT OR FANTASY?

1959! It sure sounds like ancient history when you think about it, doesn't it? I guess it was a while back and a lot of you probably don't remember most of the spine tingling details. And maybe you are even too young to have forgotten what was really going on. This section is about remembering. If you lived in the Fifties, it's a refresher course. But if you weren't so lucky, this chapter will take you right back there.

The Fifties sure was a different world. The clothes, the hair, the cars, the guys and girls, were all much more attractive. The leisure suit hadn't even been invented, polyester was a precious fabric and the energy crisis meant a car heater that broke while you were parking.

The meaning of words has changed a lot, too, since that great time. That's what this chapter's really about. You've heard all these words before, in school, at home, or around skid row, so you probably know what they mean today. This dictionary will fill you in on what they meant to everybody in the Fifties.

A 50's Dictionary

AL·CO·HOL/ālka'hál

Unidentified substance found in wine, beer, whiskey flavored toothpaste and prom punch. Frowned upon, condemned as a menace, yet consumed by parents, teachers, theologians, and politicians. Produces an euphoric effect and a sharpening of reflexes favored by drag racers and airline pilots alike. Rising birth rate on the moon following the repeal of prohibition has been attributed to its aphrodesiac effect.

Anticipated grain shortages may slow down production of **alcohol** by 1964. Government authorities fear that a reduction in the supply of alcohol could cause a revolt among an estimated 55 million teenage alcoholics. A top secret crash program to find an artificial substitute is under way in Antarctica.

— Typical teenage alcoholics

DAT·ING/dā'tín

Teen age social behavior frowned upon by many parents. Some mothers have gone so far as to say that **dating** should only be allowed after marriage. Those who fear the moral degradation produced by dating should realize the positive educational benefits. Teenagers on dates are very fond of health films such as "Muscle Madness in Miami" and driver safety films, most notably, "Hot Rod Girls."

Time on lover's lane is well spent in private late night astronomy and anatomy tutorials. **Dating** can often lead teens to drive-ins which provide modern, nutritionally balanced food products: malts, burgers, and fries.

One can safely say that America's teens are the best educated and fed in the world. All this, a result of **dating.**

— The automobile is a popular place to go on a date

DRI·VE-INS/drívè-nṣ

Restaurants in which people can eat a complete meal without ever leaving their car. This craze is literally revolutionizing the eating habits of nearly everyone. Washington nutritionists predict that **drive-ins** will completely erradicate malnutrition in America before 1961.

Sweeping **drive-ins** right now, from Seattle to New York is a new broasting process. The hamburger (bun, burger, catsup, and mustard) is cooked under great pressure in a mild soap solution, and now flies from the freezer to your car in under four minutes. What an American dream!

As a result, teenagers flock to **drive-ins** in order to save valuable time best spent studying Latin and integral calculus. **Drive-ins** for trains, airplanes, and oceanliners are under construction to allow busy travelers to eat without having to lose important time.

— Gangs often hold business meetings at drive-ins

EL·VIS/él'vís

Elvis — **Elvis** the King, the Great One. Male vocalist known primarily for his hushed and romantic recordings. While literally worshiped by America's teens, **Elvis** has increasingly incurred the wrath of American parents — because of his allegedly suggestive stage behavior.

One mother in Pittsburg, Kansas, fearful that his gyrating hip motions would impair the morals of a minor (her 13 year old daughter), has produced a television screen cover. This device is designed to block out the lower portion of the screen when **Elvis** appears on Teen Gangband. It has been endorsed by church groups and is reportedly enjoying excellent sales in Indiana, Iowa and Nebraska.

Nonetheless, the popularity of **Elvis** remains unchallenged.

— Unusually quiet Elvis fans

GANG•S/gaṅg's

Groups of teenagers dedicated to civic betterment. Modeled after community service and Christian missionary organizations, teenage **gangs** perform a multitude of volunteer services.

Often they will totally dismantle a complete stranger's car in a search for defective parts, at absolutely no charge to the owner. Their constant search for potentially dangerous, out of balance hubcaps has done much to improve our highway safety record.

Gangs usually provide free security service at football games, patrolling the parking lots for potential troublemarkers and gate crashers. Without the unselfish acts of **gangs,** our world would be a far more dangerous place to live in. We owe them our support.

— Free security service

GRE•ASE/grēá's

A hair care product designed to allow safe motoring in convertibles. Today, almost every family owns two automobiles, and at least one of those cars is a convertible. A major hazard with convertibles has been temporary blindness caused by the hair blowing across the eyes at high speeds. Accidents involving convertibles striking boats, airplanes, and lakes can be attributed to this hair problem.

The revolutionary invention of a self lubricating starch for men's hair, known by most as **grease**, has opened up motoring by convertible to those with thin, flyaway hair. What started as a safety measure is rapidly becoming a national fad. Men and women everywhere are greasing their hair. Sales of hair care products are increasing so rapidly that within two years the United States will replace Hollywood as the world's leading consumer of hair **grease**.

— Teenager about to test this new product

HOT ROD·S/hót rod's

Highly modified automobiles preferred by teenagers 33 to 1 over the best 3-speed bicycles. These vehicles can usually be spotted by their fluorescent paint jobs, simulated chrome tires, barefoot gas pedals, and cat-with-blinking-eyes turn signals.

Engines are always conscientiously modified for increased fuel economy. Common modifications (of even parent's cars) include triple 4-barrel carbs, plastic exhaust headers, pseudo-superchargers, fuel injection and cruise control. Automotive engineers predict that today's modifications will become standard features on the 1960 family car.

Also very popular with **hot rod** owners has been raising the rear end so that the car sits at a 45 degree angle in relation to the pavement. This is solely for increased visibility. Searching for aerodynamic improvement, a few concerned owners have gone so far as to put the entire body of the car on backwards. The driver looks out the former rear window, the fins cut through the air better, and top speed is increased by 50%. In two years this switch should be a factory option — if Detroit's predictions are correct.

— Hot rods always attract a crowd

JU·KE BOX/ju'ke bóx

A device designed to spin records and collect money. The juke box has brought rock and roll to the remotest regions of the country. Now almost every town (no matter how small) has at least one **juke box.** Hooter, Arizona, a rural community of 15 people, proudly boasts of five. This gives it the highest per-capita ratio of **juke boxes** in the country.

Some experts have gone so far as to predict that this device will eventually replace live music. In several years, we should expect to find **juke boxes** in busses, trains, airplanes, and golf carts, bringing the wonderful world of music to cool Americans on the move.

— Live musicians have trouble drawing crowds these days, thanks to jukeboxes

KA·NGA·ROO/ngā'róó

A dance modeled after Aborigine tribal fertility dances. The **Kangaroo** is sweeping the country today; the wild gyrations of Kangaroo dancers are whipping parents into a near frenzy.

Oklahoma law enforcement officials have suggested mandatory prison sentences for anyone caught teaching the **Kangaroo** to a minor. Ministers are quoting Revelations, contending that this "obscene" dance portends the judgment days of this earth.

Defenders of the **Kangaroo** say that the gyrating hip movements of this dance are not intentionally suggestive, but rather are designed to help people become more proficient at the hula-hoop. As yet this question is unresolved.

— Kangaroo abusers

LEA•THER/léa'ther

A new miracle fabric developed originally as a missile nose cover is becoming the fabric of choice for teenagers. Initially, only jackets were made of this material, but today teenagers enjoy the economy of **leather** ties, the style of **leather** socks and the comfort of **leather** sheets.

Automotive engineers are investigating the possibility of fabricating an entire automobile out of **leather**. The largest consumer of leather, however, is the clothing industry. Some of the new **leather** fashions enjoy regional popularity. Teens in Indiana enjoy **leather** handkerchiefs made out of old coats. Alaska's young people demand **leather** socks; **leather** bras are catching on in California.

Fearful of a shortage, scientists are working hard on a natural substitute for leather.

— Leather wearer from Indiana

TA•IL FIN/ta'íl fĭn

The automobile was originally designed to end the problems of stampeding horses and street sanitation. Although the automobile has completely transformed the look of America, automotive design progress has been extremely limited until the 1950's.

The invention of the **Tailfin** by German space scientist Warner Von Voom, has been heralded as the most impressive development in automobile safety since the invention of the solid rubber punctureproof tire. Experts predict that the **tailfin's** dramatic effect on high speed stability will cut the highway death rate 40%.

The stabilizing effects of **tailfins**, combined with the increased maneuverability produced by steering wheel spinners, heralds a new era of safe high speed motoring in America.

— Tailfins could have prevented this accident

T V/tv

Reading books has been favored by educators for many years, but recent studies indicate that television will soon replace reading altogether. Today, books are usually bought only for flattening corsages and holding windows open.

Our present revolution in education is just beginning. Educators favor **T V** viewing 5 to 1 as an educational medium. For example, University of Arkansas third year law students now receive extra credit in Advanced Criminal Procedure 611 for watching "Dragnet" and the "Untouchables." This year the most popular topics for doctoral dissertations at the University of Oklahoma are the television programs "Hopalong Cassidy" and "The Lone Ranger."

Some politicians, among them Senator Joe McCarthy and Vice President Richard Nixon have introduced bills in Congress providing for mandatory viewing of "Leave it to Beaver," in an effort to combat growing delinquency in pre-teenagers.

— Educational television

FROM NERD TO GREASER–
– In Six Easy Steps

In which a meek and timid high school senior, Melvin Q. Luzier, who hasn't had a date in three years or even a kind word from a chick in two, is transformed into a man among men.

Your Personal
Road To Coolness

Follow this simple, step-by-step pictorial essay on cool-back-to-school threads and you, too, can terrorize your enemies and inflame passion in the heart of every woman you meet (including your enemy's girlfriend).If "Nowhere Melvin" can do it, then so can you.

The Basic Nerd *A guy like you?*

Typical American Nerd, otherwise known as jerk, goon, goof, or creep. He carries a harmonica case to school; practices four hours a day, and an extra 2 hours on Friday and Saturday nights.

Note goofy look and 8th grade arithmetic book. This Nerd's eyesight is so bad he's asked the drinking fountain out for a date three times this week. Any normal Nerd would have given up after the second turndown. His specs are broken so often by his affectionate classmates that he orders them by the dozen.

Step 1 – The Semi-Nerd

Remove uncool, unhip broken glasses. Replace with studly sunglasses.

Shades help the Nerd's myopic vision, but he still looks like a geek, maybe even a goon. Bowtie is only suitable for Sunday school. Who needs books?

Step 2 – Basic Jerk

Get rid of books, harmonica, and bowtie. Replace black socks and white shoes with black shoes and white socks.

Nerd is getting spruced up, maybe even a little bit cool. White socks and Mexican fence climbing shoes build confidence. Books, bowtie and harmonica case are home with Mother — where they belong!

Step 3 – Average Senior

Trade baggy whites to night morgue attendant for blue jeans owned by a stiff.

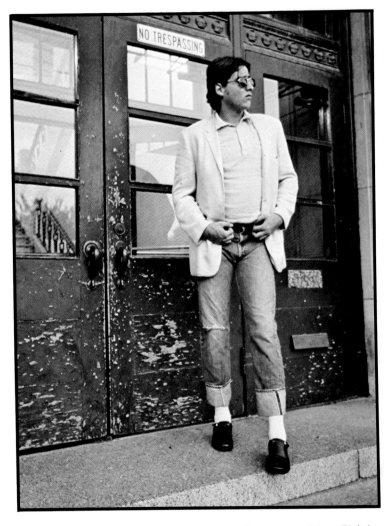

Nerd is getting there — maybe ready for a rumble. Chicks are looking him over. Parents are starting to worry. Grades are declining daily — all good signs!

Step 4 – Delinquent

Trade pink checked shirt to illegal alien for white T-shirt. Soak hair for six hours in whale oil.

Our Nerd is no longer a geek or a goon. Not quite cool yet but this guy is definitely getting there. He's bought a steering wheel spinner; plans to steal a car to go with it. Has given up brushing his teeth.

Step 5 – Potential Runaway

Trade father's favorite $95 white coat to whino for bottle of imported Indiana vino and 3 packs of cigarettes. Roll cigarette pack in sleeve.

Cigarette burns have ruined all his parent's upholstery — police call nightly to make sure he's in bed. He has two dates per night, every day of the week. This guy is not one to mess with.

Step 6 – Cool

Rip off leather jacket from blind, crippled Hells Angel in charity hospital. Purchase autographed Elvis comb and one case of Army surplus jeep grease.

Our man is ready for reform school. Girls love the sound of leather, demand to ride in the back seat. Police are now afraid to call. Parents have moved and left no forwarding address. This guy is **cool!**

The New Man — *Super Cool*
A True Story

Since completing our course, Melvin's life has dramatically changed. A few weeks ago at school he was so afraid of having food put down his back and other bodily abuse, that he ate his lunch alone in the men's room.

Today, with the increased confidence given by his new cool look, he is captain of the football team, president of his class and now dates both the head cheerleader and the principal's wife.

His personal vendetta against his former tormentors has led to false arrests in 7 states and 3 alleged violations of the Mann Act. Now when Melvin goes to lunch, everyone else eats in the bathroom.

You Can Do It Too!

— Virgin Senior.

A GUIDE TO DATING

Since almost 90% of you are illiterate (if government studies are correct), we have prepared a visual guide to cool and uncool dating including . . .

Meeting The Parents

Leaving Home

The Drive-In

Watching A 3-D Movie

Kissing Goodnight

First Base

Meeting The Parents

Second Base

Leaving Home

Third Base

The Drive-In

Fourth Base

Watching A 3-D Movie

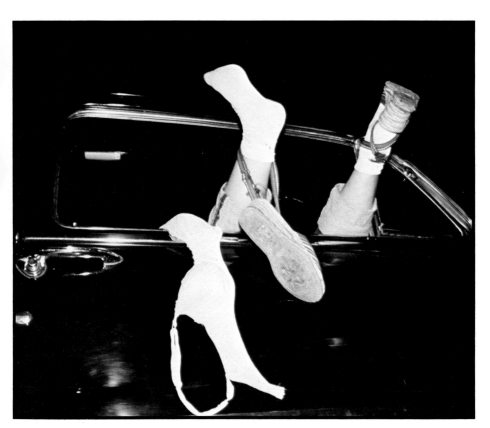

Fifth Base

Kissing Goodnight

ADVERTISING

PRAEGER

A CHAIN IS ONLY
AS STRONG AS
ITS WEAKEST LINK
(OUR MOTTO)

THE 1955 *Fleetland Special Electra-Stream Deluxe*

THE AUTOMOBILE OF THE FUTURE

"28 MONTHS AHEAD OF ITS TIME" *MOTOR & TRACK WEEKLY*

RODRIGUEZ

of

MADRID

On Enemy Turf!

A Rival Gang jumps you —
You're ready for them —
Because you carry the best . . .

RODRIGUEZ

Knife makers to
The Conquistadores

(Fine Cutlery since 1452)

A Contest

Yes, but only for the cool!

You Can Be
A Winner!

After you complete this book, send us a before and after photograph — the former being your old nerdy self, the latter being the **new** cool guy or gal produced by this book.

No Cash Prizes

The person whom we feel has made the most dramatic improvement will receive, absolutely free of charge, 10 copies of the **Grease Guide to Coolness** worth at least $39.95.

Please . . .

Send 100 **Grease Guide to Coolness** covers along with your before and after photographs to:

Comrad Leonid Frogsheu
The Russian Embassy
Anchorage, Alaska
67124

(This contest is limited to employees, friends and relatives of the publisher and is void in the United States, Canada and the remainder of the known world.)